Exploring Infinity

Solving the Mysteries of Time and Space

AF140828

To the lovely lady who always puts people first, I love you, Isolde

Stephen Janusz

Exploring Infinity

Solving the Mysteries of Time and Space

Dedication

This book is dedicated to all the people of the world that are, were, or will be, physically or mentally handicapped, because in infinity they are all healed.

May, 2013

Bibliografische Information der Deutschen Nationalbibliothek:
Die Deutsche Nationalbibliothek verzeichnet diese Publikation in der
Deutschen Nationalbibliografie; detaillierte bibliografische Daten
sind im Internet über http://dnb.dnb.de abrufbar.

© 2013 Stephen Janusz

Herausgeber: SchoonMediaServices GbR
Illustrationen: Ulrike Schoon

Herstellung und Verlag: BoD – Books on Demand, Norderstedt
ISBN: 978-3-7322-4234-4

CHAPTERS AT A GLANCE

PREFACE

"We all live lives of quiet desperation", someone once said. Why is that? Most probably because we poor creatures don't know where we are, how we got here, and don't know where we are going. This humble book will try to explain, or at least try to rationalize, the answers to these questions. The great minds of the human race, people like Confucius, Buddha, Aristotle, Socrates, Plato, Galileo, Newton, Goethe, Heisenberg, Einstein, and lately, Hawking, have all contributed to the effort. Some call it physics, others, Metaphysics. The great thinkers used measurable data, logic, scientific methods, and intuition. Some are atheists, others are religious, some switched from one position to the other.

Playwrights and poets also contribute to science unknowingly, from the aesthetic realm. They express their view of what is and isn't real. "To be or not to be?" from Shakespeare, probably is as meaningful of a scientific question as "what is a "quark"? Current scientific evidence shows indirectly that entities are darting in and out of existence on the sub-atomic level. This is science. But religion is also conceived by us as humans. So if one tries to answer unsolvable questions, one tends to lean in the direction of a religious explanation. See Chapter 5, how religion and science tend to meet somewhere in infinity.

Every thought needs a thinker. The creation of the universe must have come from a thinker. The levels of existence may start with pure thought! These concepts are an out-of-the box experience. Just remember we are all beginners on this subject. In the following pages, we will explore the ways infinity can take us to places we have never gone before. Remember Star Trek analogies, we shall see that again. Infinitely small is just as astounding as infinitely large. Similarly, the sister of infinity, eternity, has similar characteristics: eternity goes on in the past as well as the future.

Infinity requires a discussion of mathematical concepts, our planet, evolution, the big bang, the communion of spirits, what will the future be like, and how religion and science intersect somewhere in infinity. Let us differentiate "eternity" from "infinity". Eternity is infinity in terms of time. Infinity is everything. It includes time, space, matter, energy, and all abstracts, including good, bad, strong, weak, etc. This theory by the way, has no "strings" attached. (1) In this book, We will attempt to keep it "light". We do not pretend to know all the answers, because after all, Aristotle once said, "He who says "I know", is a fool. I am not a fool, because I know that I don't know." But please read this book all the way to the end, to get the true meaning. So "Beam me up, Scotty"!

CHAPTER ONE

Where does the Universe Come From?

This is our story. Steve's grandfather was building something strange and wonderful in his workshop. He vaguely remembers because he was very young and only saw it once. It was a perpetual motion machine, Victor said in his broken English. This got Steve started. He had many long hours with his grandfather talking about time, space, and God.

"If you throw a ball of matter into space at the speed of light, it will turn into pure energy." This is a quote once attributed to Albert Einstein. Funny, but I just thought what if you reversed the process? What if you took that energy, and slowed it down BELOW the speed of light? It should turn back into matter! Bingo! That's the creation of the Universe! Now, imagine you have pure energy. Imagine it picks up such speed surpassing the speed of light that causes it to dart in and out of existence on a quantum level. I postulate that it can be compared with the speed of "thought" or "spirit". We will soon discuss the nature of thought in following chapters. This is leaving our three dimensional universe. (2)

Then go back to the original assumption: Start out with "spirit" or "thought": take "thought", slow it down to the speed of light ("Let there be light"!-Sound familiar?), it becomes "energy", slow it down below the speed of light, it becomes "matter" (The Universe)!

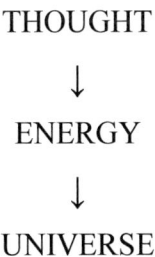

THOUGHT

↓

ENERGY

↓

UNIVERSE

Perhaps an even bigger question is "why did it come? Who's doing the thinking"? We will discuss evolution, "The Big Bang" theory, and other theories later on. But if you can think, you can move mountains.

According to Hawking, the Universe could be neither created nor destroyed, just "BE". (3)

CHAPTER TWO

Math has Infinity in it!

$$y = x^2$$

It is said that parallel lines meet at infinity. In Einstein's, then Hawking's Space-Time Continuum, conventional mathematics, although theoretically correct, can be irrational at times.

That's why the invention of quantum mechanics was necessary, to bring real world into the study of mathematics. But mathematics still is the perfect science and plays a large role in defining terms in a logical frame of reference. Algebraic concepts and philosophical concepts are similar. A = B is similar in form to "All men are mortal". Math shows examples of how infinity is staring right at us, if we only had an eye to see and an ear to listen.

Have you ever heard of a differential? No matter. The rest of this book will discuss infinitely large and small, infinitely long and short, all concepts that cannot with our less than infinite mental powers, be grasped. But math has an example of infinity already, in simple geometry- the circle! It has no beginning, no end. Ever wonder why the planets and the suns are round? It is the natural state of things that the universe of planets and stars uses spheres. It is a product of the mysterious force of gravity, where all parts of an object are equidistant from the center. Even in your blood stream, things are round. Anything falling apart, including cancer, gets odd shapes. In infinity, the circle is the natural state.

But it is not that simple. Let's get back to the differential, or the first derivative. In the 16th century, in Europe, two men almost simultaneously but independently, came up with differential calculus, the math part of science that sends rockets to the moon. It determines situations that only can be guessed at by ordinary math. But it shows that the infinite exists! Sir Gottfried von Leibnitz and Sir Isaac Newton, esteemed mathematicians, independently came up with formulae using a simple graph and a parabola that demonstrated that the slope of a smaller and smaller right triangles via x and y axes. Delta X approaches zero. The triangle that defined the slope shrank to the extent that it coincides with the POINT. Since a POINT has no length, width, or depth, it does not exist in the three dimensional universe; yet it does exists because it performs a function! Another example of the 1st derivative is that it takes the function, velocity, and derives acceleration, precisely and mathematically.

Infinity is shown in math by the repeating decimal, taken from fractions like 1/3. It equals .333333... ad infinitum. but is perfectly represented by the fraction. Another example is pi. Take the circumference of a circle, divide it by its diameter, and you get pi, approximately 22/7.But it is a non- repeating, non- terminating decimal. Scientists have taken it out past 600 decimals, with no end in sight. Still other examples are the square root concept, and the irrational square root of a negative number. Almost magic isn't it?

"How many angels can sit on a head of a pin?"my mother used to say. You can bisect a line an infinite number of times, and you still have some line left. If a number divided by one is the same number, what is a number divided by zero? In the function, $y = 1/x$, where x approaches "0", y approaches infinity.

Math allows us to play games with infinity. Quantum mechanics was invented to try to make sense of math in the physical world. They are still making new theories.

The equation for the symbol of infinity is described below:(4)

1.   The lemniscate, also called the lemniscate of Bernoulli, is a polar curve whose most common form is the locus of points

the product of whose distances from two fixed points (called the foci) a distance $2a$ away is the constant a^2. This gives the Cartesian equation where both sides of the equation have been squared. Expanding and simplifying then gives below.

$$\left(x^2 + y^2\right)^2 = 2c^2\left(x^2 - y^2\right).$$ $$r^2 = 2a^2 \cos 2\theta$$

OR

2.   The reason the symbol of infinity is what it is, comes from way back in the cultures of ancient mathematicians, It is in the "collective consciousness " of the human race.

The following is a demonstration of mathematical principles of the first derivative showing we have a function AFTER DEATH.

Below is a sketch of a type of parabola $y = x^2$.

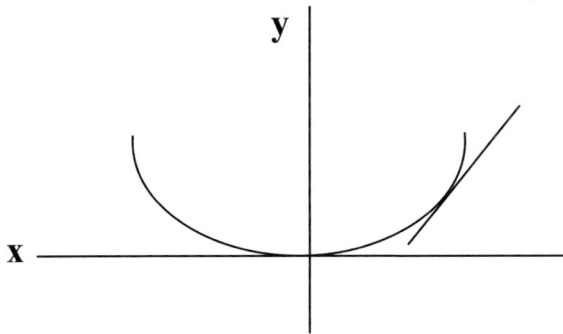

The slope m (as in y = mx +b) of a line tangent to any point on the curve is determined by a formula developed by Gottfried von Leibnitz of Germany and Sir Isaac Newton of Great Britain in the 16th Century. The function starts out as

$$y = x^2.$$

Only when the change in y divided by the change in x is INFINITLY small can one determine the slope of that line tangent to the curve at that point.

$$y = x^2$$

is the function, a parabola, our current life add a change dy and a change dx

$$y + dy = (x + dx)^2$$

$$y + dy = x^2 + 2xdx + (dx)^2$$

subtract the function $- y = - x^2$

$$Dy = 2xdx + (dx)^2$$

Divide thru by dx,

$$dy/dx = 2x + dx$$

let dx approach 0

$$dy/dx = 2x + 0$$

therefore,

$$dy/dx = 2x$$

is the derivative — a new function, a straight line

$$y = 2x$$

at our death (flatlined).

The first derivative, the straight line function which determines the slope of the line tangent to the curve at that point, ends up as the function y = 2x. This resulted when an infinitely small slope (dy/dx) was formed. Therefore a form of INFINITY exists after the relationship dy/dx approaches 0.

SOUL = y

BODY = x

Dx (change in x) approaches 0

Explanation:

The graph above omits the x- y axis for simplicity. Y is the value of the soul (vertical axis). X is the value of our body (horizontal axis). Just as the slope exists at a point where the line is tangent to the curve, so also does the soul exist when the body goes to zero.

The value of y is dependent on the value of x. I believe that the human race has an ultimate function as well. If what results when we live, is the function of how we behave during our lives (the original equation, y = x squared) , what happens to our souls after we die is determined by our value x at the time our death occurs (the first derivative, when x approaches 0 and the new function is y=2x). We do not go out of existence when we die; dy/dx just approaches infinity, it is a point that is infinitely small, and that is the mystery.

CHAPTER THREE

Mother Earth-Father Time

Let's start with Father Time. Time is relative. Anybody know what a "nano" is? It is one billionth of something. In distance, it is one billionth of a length of measure; for example, nanometer, one billionth of a meter, or .000000001m. In time, a nano-second is one billionth of a second.

I was standing outside a train station waiting for a bus one time, and I had some bread crumbs to feeds the pigeons, invariably there in public places. I threw some out and I noticed one bird flew to it and caught it in mid-flight. Now how did she do that? It dawned on me that some creatures that are smaller than us seem to be aware of things quicker than us because they measure time in their own minds in a different measure than us. Computers have created the time scale in which the time duration of a simulated event is greater than the actual time duration of the event under study. (5)

Perhaps they measure time in proportion to their "size" relative to us. If you have a dog, you know that example of how quickly it can grasp the frisbee. Postulating the example- A bird is one tenth of our size, so it may have ten times as much time in its own "world" to catch the crumb in flight. A smaller creature- take a fly. Notice how a fly avoids bumping into things at high speed or getting caught if you just casually swipe at it? It may not be just reflex, but a thought process- he sees you coming in slower motion because one second for us may seem like a minute to him.

It may not be size but lifespan. Perhaps the lifespan of a creature is inversely proportional to its awareness of time, for example, a fruit fly lives one day, but to him, it may seem to be a 70 year lifetime. Now take the opposite approach-if you are a larger being or have a longer lifespan, you see things go by faster. The longer you live, the faster time seems to go by.

Now take this rather absurd (remember "infinity" is incomprehensible) example out to infinity. The infinitely small or short lived being has time slowed down so much that its time seems not to move at all. An atom, if it were alive, would view an atomic chain reaction as if it took billions of years, although to us it happens in a split second.

To an infinitely large or long lived being, the "Big Bang" in our Universe then would have time all move so fast that it is all over in an instant. Us wee little creatures in our large Universe think it is happening for billions of years, just like that atom previously referenced.

Take this all the way out to infinity. The infinitely small hasn't even started its time, so it is virtually standing still, whereas the infinitely large sees all time so fast that it appears all at the same time, or instantly. So absurdly, "time" neither exists for the infinitely large or the infinitely small. The large is especially interesting.

If the greatest thing in infinity were a conscious "being", it would see the birth and death of the universe as just a point. So it lives outside of time. Maybe this is how "heaven" could be infinitely long yet not boring! But we are getting ahead of ourselves.

Another concept of time is that it is like an 8mm film, which only moves when "they" run the projector. But we will discuss this in Chapter 14, "Universe # 429".

As for Mother Earth, we are all spinning around in a universe that appears immeasurably large with billions of stars in our galaxy alone. But in terms of infinity, it may be so small that it may be a system no bigger than an amoeba in a blood stream of a fantastically larger system. And we may be no more than specks on the skin of one of these tiny amoeba. Maybe the universe is no more than a molecule- size element in this system. Remember, nothing is ever the smallest or largest, just approaching it. On the other scale, infinitely small, maybe within our own body, there is a blood stream of tiny little universes we cannot see because they are infinitely too small for us to see.

In physics, the universe goes on and on. In math, it is like a non-repeating, non-terminating decimal.

CHAPTER FOUR
Thought-A new Reality?

Are our thoughts really in existence? Thought is a great dynamic force with tremendous power. A simple atom radiates an electromagnetic field or EMF. These "vibrations" (for lack of a better word) are sent out to the physical world extending outward to the non-physical world. The very fabric of space-time that makes up the universe is composed of "threads". It is ever changing and we change with the tiniest thought. (6).

According to Edey Calwell Sanders, in the early 1990′s, Dr. Candice Pert made an amazing discovery that tells you exactly why you manifest abundance, health, relationships, etc., or why you do not.

"While Dr. Pert was the chief molecular biologist for the National Institutes of Health she discovered that your thoughts are real, physical things. Your thoughts become molecules the instant you think them and, as a deliberate attractor, you need to know how those molecules interact with your body.

Every time you have a thought, (point –the "thought is not what happens to it, it came first)……your hypothalamus (a "control center" near the base of your brain) transforms that thought into millions of neuropeptides (amino acids) which represent the dominant emotion associated with that thought. Your thought becomes a molecular messenger of emotion! And then your bloodstream is flooded with these neuropeptides.

When in your bloodstream, these neuropeptides, into which your thought transformed, actually insert themselves into your cells. Each neuropeptide interlocks with a special receptacle (made just for it) on your cell's membrane – just like a lock fitting into a keyhole. And then that amino acid is absorbed by your cell. Over time, Dr. Pert found, your cells develop more and more special receptacles for the neuropeptides to which they are most exposed. And over time your cells create a self-fulfilling emotional prophecy for you. Your cells begin to crave the neuropeptides to which they are most exposed (and have built all the receptacles for) and they "tell" your hypothalamus to produce them". (7)

This idea that a "thought" is physical may be confused with the word "memory", which is physical. It remains a mystery as to the nature of a spiritual "thought" and a physical manifestation of that thought. It is tied with the concept of our brain having the Id, the Ego, and the Super Ego, as Freud describes it, as we will discuss.

In the great religions of the world, thought and consciousness are paramount. A great religious figure is reported to have said, "if you even have lust in your heart for a woman outside of your marriage, you have already committed adultery with her". Is this just imagination or is this a reality? Is it possible that this concept can be taken literally, in a dimension in a parallel universe where it is metaphysically true, has actually happened? Someone says if you die in your dream, your heart stops. Is the thought like a spirit that can become something tangible like the energy that became matter (see introduction)? When you "burn in Hell", is this hell only figurative but as well, an actual place in a different dimension? Another example: "trans-substantiation ". In the Catholic Church, this means the changing of bread and wine into "Body and Blood of Christ". This happens in that spiritual dimension that we cannot see until we go there. "Metaphysical" is a term in philosophy, that means above the physical. "Will power" in a Metaphysical world is an actual substance. Add to that the concept of "sin". If you "sin", that part of your "soul" gets burnt for it in another dimension where it is a substance, an actual body in this other, Metaphysical world. We think "thought" is only intelligent when done by our species. But maybe not. Philosophers have meditated over how a spider spins his web for a millions of years in the same way. This thought-out plan of the spider, a natural mutation of the survival of the fittest, is a skill bestowed on a species to do something in the best possible way by an intelligent designer, a perfect architect. Birds could fly south for the winter by choice thought not by a controller like robots. In infinity all things are possible. Perhaps all have causes, nothing can be left out. All effects have a cause. We already came to a conclusion in Chapter One that THOUGHT causes the universe.

CHAPTER FIVE

Science and Religion meet in Infinity

Did you ever consider the phenomenon of miracles? Throughout the ages, things like healing through prayer, laying of the hands, invocations, have been manifesting themselves. Miracles have normally been accompanied by the power of positive thinking. I define a "miracle" as "human brain waves synchronized with the power the universe". Jesus walking on water, the sun changing colors (Fatima), the virgin birth, the resurrection and ascension, are all what we call "metaphysical" events, scoffed at by atheists, but believed by religious people. I offer a third alternative: these events can be real, in time, but not known by our time. Let's get back to Star Trek. We whimsically accept that in science fiction, "Beam me up, Scotty", is considered as a possibility. It was called a "transporter" and the thing it did was Teleportation". So why cannot we believe in teleporting, time travel, or the existence of other dimensions? Our discussion of "heaven" is so limited in words, that we are stopped in our tracks making any connection between the existence of the "miraculous" and our 5 senses. Jesus was the only Biblical figure who claimed to be "God", and was killed for it. He said, "Father, forgive them, for they know not what they do". They just didn't know any better. Books are coming out now with "life after death" testimonials of what was previously scoffed at. Science thinks the brain seeing the "light" at death is just neurons misfiring, plausible when energy is given off. But it could really be the Metaphysical event of life coming after death. Television, telephones, internet, and microwave machines are all common place today. If you placed them into a primitive society they would be considered miraculous. In infinity, teleportation, telepathy, telekinesis, and time travel may SOME DAY become as accepted as television. Who's to say if great inspiration is not sent by an intelligensia greater than us from a distant world or time?

Let us discuss the concept of "empirical observation" as a scientific tool. Philosophy is a science that is not earth grounded like physics is. Physics is the study of what we see in empirical observation. But there are gliches to the certainty of physics, for example, Heisenberg's "Uncertainty Principle". This principal stated that you cannot really measure anything accurately, because in the act of measurement, you change it.

Plato, Greek philosopher, had a little insight into the fallacy of "empirical observation" in his allegorical story about the "Cave of Shadows". The story goes something like this: there is a cave. There are prisoners chained in this cave, unable to turn their heads. All they can see is the wall of the cave. Behind them burns a fire. Between the fire and the prisoners there is a passage, along which puppeteers can walk. The puppeteers, who are behind the prisoners, hold up puppets that cast shadows on the wall of the cave. The prisoners are unable to see these puppets, the real objects, that pass behind them. What the prisoners see and hear are shadows and echoes cast by objects that they do not see. The shadows are their REALITY. The point is: what we see. hear, feel, touch and taste is not the real things, just the SHADOWS, which we interpret as being the reality. On the other hand, Philosophers study "Metaphysics", the science that involves the study of the supernatural realities. Supernatural realities can only be understood if we use abstract logical arguments, for example, "all men are mortal, John Smith is a man, therefore John Smith is mortal". This is an example of Deductive Reasoning. From this we can logically reason to the existence of Metaphysical realities. Inductive reasoning is not as definitive, but is also relevant. The first statement "All men are mortal", is inductive, because it argues from the case of the the many examples confirming the conclusion, Since every human being we see dies, this give us the conclusion that all men are mortal, the "miracle" of Jesus, notwithstanding. What gives us the power to even think about something without it becoming a reality in some form?

I believe that in infinity, every "thought" is recorded and takes on a "real" body in infinity. You may achieve NIRVANA as a real place in a different reality. Our universe was thought to be empty. Now science has discussed the possible existence of "dark matter" to describe a presence of what we formerly thought to be the empty vacuum of space. I believe that eventually, science and religion will join forces. But I think in our present state of intelligence, the "God Particle" recently discovered cannot be fully understood.

According to Skylark and Funderberg:

> "In science the majority believe that the universe was created in an "explosion" (no laws governing explosions back then) of matter and anti-matter called the Big Bang... Others might call this the work of God, and scientists with all matters of statistics and proof needed to make this a recognizable theory, none have been able to explain why the Big Bang occurred in the first place. There must have been some external force... that is basic physics. Sounds like God's hand at work does is not? Coincidence? NO! Another theory of science would be the THEORY of evolution, the process of slight mutation in the cells in plants and later animals. Originally life began in a primordial soup (another theory) by a RANDOM combination of chemicals that miraculously sprang forth into the first single-celled organisms we know and love today. Maybe it was lightning? Or maybe it was random... it is a big universe... but I don't think so. In truth, randomness does not exist, everything has a cause to do what it is doing. From there with quite apparently random mutations, those single-celled organisms slowly became more complex. Was life not good single-celled? unlimited food and energy. What drove them forward? And from then on, slowly moving forward into the next step. The previous system obviously worked before, otherwise they would have died out ". (8)

I think that the truth is, our science is still improving and realizing more and more that what we formerly thought to be absolute truth is only what we perceive to be trueby our limited faculties. "Science" once thought the Earth was the center of the Universe, and the sun rotated around us.

CHAPTER SIX

Where did We Come From?

Someone once said, "you give a million monkeys a million typewriters over a million years, and they will write all the works of Shakespeare". These accidental events in time define the infinite possibilities if you believe in "dumb" evolution. You need no "designer". If "natural selection" occurs by accidental mutations, given an infinite amount of time, this is a good argument, since in infinity, there is room for all events. But who is making the "natural selections"? What is "nature" to begin with?

Evolution and natural selection are defined as changes that occur in events due to needs in the environment of the recipient, for example, the horny toad frog develops a long tongue because he is trying for generations to reach food (insects). The successful changes stick, the non-successful ones wither away. Mankind, the ultimate species, came about by a series of selections that survived- it's all about WINNING, as Charlie Sheen might say. All of man's intelligence came about by an accidental or environmentally produced "need" to evolve. So homo sapiens were produced by a "dumb" evolutionary process.

An argument against this might be, how can a "dumb" evolution make a "smart" creature. The DNA within makes the species. I love cars. But can an automobile build itself by accident? How much more likely is it for a living thing like a horny toad frog to get its DNA purely by a series of accidents? Especially if it comes from a "dumb" evolution. For every effect, there is a cause. If something non-intelligent produced us, is it consistent with the concept that the maker of something cannot be at a lower level than the thing it makes? It would presume that we are not really intelligent at all. So why should we talk to each other at all, we are all dumb!

So, since we think we are intelligent, that theory cannot stand. The "parent processor" that made us must be more intelligent than we are. In other words, we have the "Creator's" DNA! Or do you really want to believe that we have the great works of Shakespeare by accident? We will discuss later what should happen if a million human beings progress a billion years.

Now the question at hand: Which came first-the chicken or the egg? Let us first define the "chicken" and the "egg". The chicken is the organism that has certain features, one of which is, it has stuff inside it which makes it a unique species, DNA.

The "egg" is an entity which is composed of a shell within which lies the substance which resembles the uniqueness of its parent and will follow the path of the DNA it is given

Carl Sagen showed in experiments that when gases are assembled in a vessel and "sparked" (Light or electricity) a strange brown pigment forms. They are the beginnings of amino acids and "nucleotides". (9)

It is given that in science, life's origin itself is not known; logic concludes that it arrived either on earth or coming from space to earth. But the consensus of scientists is that the order of appearance in evolution is the cell, then protein, then genetics. Genetics is the "genes" and DNA.

The key is "replication", which is the reproduction of the same genetic likeness. (10)

Since replication needs genes to bring about a matching continuation, it stands to reason that there was an organism first, whose cells (which is not the egg) retained their 1dentity by either developing or being given, "genes", improving the species.

The egg, which comes out of the chicken, has genetic material in it, grows and replicates. How would it be if a baby was born before its parents? Ergo, the chicken came before the egg.

As for evolution, let us consider that an Entity smarter than "man" is responsible for us being here as intelligent entities, and for the sake of argument, call this Entity the Intelligent Designer (ID).

Atheists say there is no God. But we don't have to believe we are the only creatures in the universe with intelligence to be atheists, do we? Unless to be an atheist, you must believe that you are caused by a dumb evolutionary process.

Speaking of evolution, an Englishman, James Churchward, published "The Lost Continent of Mu". This was allegedly some land mass in the Pacific that approximately 13,000 years ago, was an earthly paradise, with no savagery, no sin, etc. It was thought to be the legendary continent of Atlantis that disappeared due to earthquakes, floods, natural calamities, and was swallowed up with 50 million square miles of water rolling over it. (10)

An alternative for where we came from is that we came from another heavenly body or "stardust". We also could have been planted by another race of vastly more advanced beings, perhaps even by our own species that left this planet eons ago, out of necessity or design. Given infinity, all events can happen. It is wonderful that we have the consciousness to even think of this. The human species has infinite potential. The Biblical explanation of Adam and Eve answers not the question of "where did we come from ?", but rather, "why"?

CHAPTER SEVEN

The Big Bang Upgraded

Let us say that theory is itself subject to be "exploded". My view: the universe cannot have a beginning obviously, otherwise it is not infinite by definition. Saying there was an actual start of the universe, implying it happened only once, is an old theory displaced by "Cyclic Universe". (11)

What is the "Big Bang"? The "Big Bang" or its reverse, the old definition of singularity, is a theory proposed in the western scientific circles, that proposes that the universe in the beginning, was all gases that were brought together by gravity. This massive amount became so tightly packed that at one point, they had to explode (nuclear fusion/fission), sending forth all the stars and planets that eventually became the Milky way, the Andromeda galaxy, etc, all of our universe. Eventually, it might stop expanding, start being pulled together again, and become a Black Hole so massive that light cannot escape it. This dense material, the whole universe condensed into the size of a baseball (literally), is called "singularity".

Far Eastern circles have a different viewpoint. I met a Buddhist monk once, who believes the universe of stars flow through a kind of ethereal tunnel/vein submerged in a "plasma" as blood corpuscles flow through the blood of an enormous Being. The modern scientists call it dark matter now, so everybody is going in the same direction. There is no definable beginning to this plasma flow, i.e., no "Big Bang". The galaxies speed up as they go through the "vein" of flow; as the, they round the bend they appear to be going into a "black hole", but maybe it is really a "capillary" leading to another vein. Thinking micro instead of macro, maybe our own veins contain universes as previously discussed, Infinity has no size boundaries. Go watch "Men in Black" one more time. Nuclear fission can take place on a small scale like in a pound of uranium, small nuclear bomb made by man, or on a large scale, like in a universe! The "God particle, or "Higgin's Boson", the latest scientific discovery in Europe, identifies an entity that facilitates mass, and consequently, the universe. This concept can be interpreted as the cause of the universe regardless if through a bang or a flow. The point is that, in infinity, there doesn't have to be a beginning, but rather a continuation of causes and effects.

CHAPER EIGHT

Singularity of Man and Machine

"Singularity" traditionally means that inside a black hole, there is a point where the curvature of light becomes bent inward through gravity.

It becomes total and cannot escape. (12)

But there is a new definition. One of the greatest innovations of the 20th century was the invention of the computer. Computers think in terms of x's and o's just like a tic-tac-toe game. Switches going on and off. But the combination of light changes and coding has accumulated just like the proverbial "million monkeys" example sited earlier when discussing a "dumb evolution". Now we have developed a million times more capacity in data processing than the computers built in the mid 20th century.

At the same time, our average age as a race, is older,

due to modern science; bionics has been advancing very quietly replacing body parts through electronics and hydraulics. Other countries, like Japan, have taken the lead in making robots that simulate human motion. Since the manufacture of the heart "pacemaker", we have been turning people in "hybrids". The brain, however is so complicated and mysterious, it has been harder to improve when malfunctioning. Therefore, human advances in neurological science have been slow. Just the opposite is happening with robots because of computer science. Now a robot can be made that walks, talks, responds, has sensors to "see". As a matter of fact, has all senses, writes, sings, dances, and solves problems, like playing chess. Add synthetic skin and voila! - a synthetic human is represented. Couple this with a negative birth rate in advanced countries, and an aging population and you get a "perfect storm". Estimates have been made that by the year 2047, if we continue this effort, we will reach "singularity". Singularity now means we will not know the difference between robots and humans, that quantities and qualities of the human and the robot will reach equality. We are witnessing the decline of the human and the rise of the "machines", the "terminator" and the "vacuum cleaner" will have equal place in society with "The "Nelsons". If not now, for sure, in infinity.

CHAPTER NINE
Armageddon

The coming of the "end of the world" has been forecasted by many philosophers, including Nostradamus in the 16th Century. This is theoretically possible, just like 50 years before the TITANIC sank, a book was written describing in great detail how it happened. In the Book of Revelations in the Judeo-Christian Bible, there is a whole passage devoted to Armageddon, the name of a place in the Middle East. Discussion is made of the falling of the stars, earthquakes, "fire and brimstone"(brimstone can be created by fire equivalent to a nuclear calamity), darkness, weeping and the gnashing of teeth, etc. In the Holy Bible, New Testament, the quote is, "the sun will be darkened, and the moon will not give its light; the stars will fall from Heaven, and the powers of the heavens will be shaken". (13)

A result of WW II was the creation of a never ending conflict. The State of Israel was installed in 1948 via United Nations charter, on the land previously held by the religious people called the Palestinians. This area of land, Armageddon, is between current Moslem countries of Egypt and Jordan. The Palestinians in 1948 were forced to leave their homes abruptly, which opened a political wound that never healed to this day. The Judeo-Christian religion claims this land around the city of Jerusalem

from thousands of years before. Throughout my lifetime, tribulation never ceases over the possession of this land. A billion Moslems sympathize with the Palestinian cause, the Western powers sympathize with the Hebrew cause. This would not cause the end of the world as we know it, but couple it with the other event that came out of WW II, the creation of the arsenals of atomic and hydrogen bombs, and you have a deadly combination.

Because of this never ending Biblical conflict, where people are willing to die for their cause, with the advent of nuclear bombs available since the end of the Cold War, and you have the makings of a calamity that could truly end the world as we know it. It is estimated that the total weapons could destroy the human race seven times over. Now terrorists have a chance to truly do their work, since the Soviet Union dissolved and their arsenals are divided and other counties are also in possession of this power of destruction in this nuclear age,

None of these factors will destroy the planet, however, because to the Earth, sun spot activity or a nuclear calamity would only put a "scab" on the surface of the planet, which would heal eventually.

The REAL end of the Earth, even if not caused by a man-made event, even if not a collision with a celestial body like a meteor or comet, will come from super nova, the dying of our star.

If you take a look at the odds, our human race will have long left our planet for other reasons. In infinity, Armageddon could be a recurring event not to be concerned about any more than our own personal death, which terminates the world for us in any case. In the distant future our race will just move on to a higher mode of transportation through the Universe or to an improved dimension. Just like an mustard seed is "destroyed" when it becomes an oak tree, it is for the greater good. In any case, "ye know not the hour, nor the day", so live each day as if it were your last.

CHAPTER TEN
Cancer-A Dying Star

Astrologers have said that looking at the stars can predict and define the important things in life. I have discovered that the death of a star has remarkable similarities with the growth of cancer, the malignancy in our bodies.

A star dies when it has used up all of its FISSIONABLE MATERI-AL. It then goes into a state called SUPER-NOVA, when it expands and consumes everything within its path. It is theorized that it then becomes a either a white dwarf or a black hole, if large enough.

Let us compare a Black Hole to a Cancer Cell. The Black Hole is just as devastating to the system around as a cancer cell. Normally, a process called aptosis takes place in the body where the good cells get rid of the dying cells when the body has a working immune system. (14)

When it doesn't, mestasis takes place, and the cells grow and suck up all matter just like a BLACK HOLE, destroying everything in its path.

The cause of cancer, then, is likened to dying cells going into SUPER NOVA. Tumors are "burned out stars".

When your good cells with vitamins and minerals absorbed into their nucleus are working, along with white blood cells vanquish the dying cell. So cancer is not and is not caused by a virus, just like AIDS is not a virus. It is rather a PROCESS, just enhanced by opportunistic viruses, like HPV, etc, coupled with a weak enough immune system to allow it to succeed.

The cure for cancer is illusive because of this fact, that it is not a disease, like influenza, but rather the inability of the host to consume enough fuel (FISSIONABLE MATERAL!) to prevent further advancement of the SUPER NOVA. The cure is in food like green vegetables containing anti-oxidants to help in absorption, etc. I hereby disclaim any expertise in medicine, but the principles of the human body, in INFINITY, are likely the same as the principles of the heavenly bodies.

Some Eastern religions believe that planets and stars have lives of their own, just like species of living organisms on Earth. For example, the Earth could in reality be a celestial giant amoeba, a one celled animal floating in a plasma (dark matter) and lives and dies after billions of years. Who is to say that us wee little "bacteria" on the surface have more of a claim to "life" than the entire planet or its mother, the star we call the "sun". We may be no more aware of the consciousness of the Earth than an ant walking on an elephant is aware of the elephant's intelligence. Incidentally, global warming may be just a defense mechanism of the Earth to get rid of the human "bacteria" that irritates it.

Furthermore, the entire universe may be just like blood platelets in a gigantic vein inside a gigantic being. All is possible in INFINITY.

CHAPTER ELEVEN

Intelligent Life on other Planets

Whether there is intelligent life on other planets is a question for the ages. I'm not quite convinced there is "intelligent" life on this planet, based on the evidence of what is going on, wars, immorality, bureaucracy, etc.

Having been to the "Rise of the Homo Sapiens" Exhibit in the Washington D.C. Smithsonian Museum of Natural History, you would think that we are indeed a product of dumb evolutionary process. There are possibly thousands of planets available in the Milky Way Galaxy that could support life. Mathematically, any reasonably intelligent person would agree that there should be a species out there that is at least equal to us. Should we be so proud to think that this whole universe is created only for us on one little corner of our galaxy? This would be philosophically the same as the pre-Galileian thinking that the earth was the center of the solar system with the sun rotating around us. Although there is the possibility that other intelligent extra-terrestrials do not look like us, there is also a possibility that they do look like us, by natural selection. Stephen Hawking discussed the uniqueness of the carbon atom and other factors that are necessary to create life like us. He concluded than it is harder than we think for us to come into existence randomly. (15)

You can either say that we are extremely fortunate, or that it is not random. Someone did it on purpose.

The existence of UFO's and intelligent life on other planets has become very popular. Many scientists speculate about the possibilities, insisting that we cannot be alone in the universe. Alien life has been the subject in movies, novels, and television for years.

Due to the intelligence shown in ancient artifacts, for example, the Aztec and Inca remains in the Western hemisphere, the race of Homo Sapiens could have been engendered by ancient visiting astronauts.

Eric von Danikan, Swiss writer, envisioned this. Also, in the Yucatan Peninsula, he contended that there are craters dating back to prehistoric times, that could have been created by rocket exhaust. (16)

It is also a common belief of many New Age religions. The Scriptures do not directly address the question of alien beings. The Bible does not explicitly confirm or deny the existence of intelligent life from other planets. Although the subject is not addressed explicitly, the Bible teaches implicitly that the only things He created with intelligence are the angels, man, and the animals as a close proximity. But if someday the extra-terrestrials come out in the open, we will not be surprised. Beam me down, Scotty! They might even be US from the future, as will be discussed in the following chapters.

CHAPTER TWELVE

Where Do You Go When You Die?

Let us define "You". In philosophy, there is "primary matter" and "substantial form". Primary matter is the essence of a thing, what makes it what it "is". Substantial form is what it looks like. The primary matter of a chair is wood. The substantial form is the configuration of the pieces held together by struts and glue or nails, that make it useful. Now, our primary matter is our soul, spirit, individuality as person. Our substantial form is the size, shape, bones, etc. Did you ever concern yourself with deformities? Don't! That is only the substantial form. In an instant in eternity it is irrelevant! The soul is eternal. Let's talk about "death" and "you".

Let's start with "near death" experiences. They are what people have experienced when seriously ill or through accident, almost lose their life. In the reports given, there runs a common thread, regardless of year, location, culture, race, or any social, cultural, genre: a tunnel, passage, movement through, until seeing a light, angelic, glowing, spiritually pleasant being, almost within reach, drawing the person into a feeling of satisfaction or happiness, only to be slowed down, and returned back to earth. "Out of body" experiences also are reported, whereby one is floating above and actually viewing one's own body and surroundings, apparently in an astral or ethereal body. In cases of actual death, no reports have been given empirically. But bodies have been measured carefully, and results seem to confirm there is indeed a loss, however slight, of mass, or weight after death, indicating that something went somewhere.

The Intelligent Designer (ID) does not have to alter the workings of nature. ID's mysterious plan includes all living things getting born, living, and dying or transforming. Trees do it, so do humans. We are aware of it perhaps more than trees. But the part of us that is not of this world, the soul, which is really "you", is released from the chains of the body. It becomes transformed into energy, then speeds up, becomes thought or spirit (see previous chapters).

"You" then goes to that place we call "heaven". This was forecasted by all religions because our destination was infused by ID in the brain so humans would not despair. Even if it hurts to die. No pain, no gain. When the acorn dies, it becomes an Oak tree.

The "thinker' that created the universe is waiting for you to become part of it in its source, where you came from. You have nothing to fear, for the good in you is eternal and infinitely existing. This is not to be confused with studies about "quarks" and other quantum dynamic particles that seem to go in and out of existence (footnote). These particles are the universe at its borders, not the final destination. The "good" returns to the spirit world in its essence, the "bad" goes to. Where do the splinters go after smoothing wood? What would YOU do with the unsalvageable splinters? Lead a good life and accept the inevitable when you must, humble yourself, and you have nothing to fear. Remember, "The eye has not seen, nor the ear heard, and the mind has not conceived of, what great things are in store for those that love Him". (17)

Ever go to a party? Why is it that we all like parties? Is it the food, the music, the booze? Science says neither matter nor energy can be either created nor destroyed, just changed from one to the other. Belief that the spirit ceases to exist when your body dies is a violation of scientific principles. So what makes you think you spirit can be destroyed?

I maintain it cannot. In infinity, all the people who have ever died or who have ever lived are together in the metaphysical reality, The party is in the spirit, thought and idea world, and the love shared by only the "good". No more fights, stage fright, shyness, just imagine the best party you ever attended, and everybody's having a Birthday! Everybody's on the team that just won the championship! We just won the World's Series/CUP!

Everybody's your friend, your counselor, your sister, brother, mother, father, friend, the linkage of mutual happiness. The greater the composition of consciousness, gathered the closer to infinity you get. That is the "heaven", the spirit world that exists in infinity.

As stated, Sigmund Freud defined the human psyche into three parts: the "id", the "ego", and the "super ego". The "id" is the part of you that desires immediate gratification in sex, food, success, etc. The "'ego" part of you negotiates and modifies itself to get along in the world of others and the environment around you. The "super ego" is the highest development in the human being. It is the part of you that sacrifices its worldly desires for the greater good, eg., "do unto others what you would have done unto you", die for your country, sacrifice for your family, etc.

I believe that the "super ego" is the part of you that lives on, in a heavenly new dimension after you die. The id and ego remain in some form on the earth where that energy continues to nourish the earth environment, with their powers of procreation. survival of the fittest, continuation of the species, etc. The bottom line is that those of us who live for the world only, will die with the world.

CHAPTER THIRTEEN

The Human Race a Billion years from Now

We discussed the unlikelihood of a "dumb" evolution creating an "intelligent" Homo Sapien race in chapter six. Let us now consider what would the human race would be like if it actually made it through the nuclear age without exterminating itself. Don't worry about the earth dying. Remember it is more likely that the Earth will always survive the human race even if gets a scab (nuclear scar) on it for a few million years. Only the death of our star, the sun, or a head on collision with a comet, or gigantic meteor, will eliminate it. I don't want to be a preacher of doom or gloom, but it is highly likely that there was a nuclear conflict and possibly we had this conflict many eons ago, several times before recorded history. So maybe we will get it right this time. Assuming all conditions continue to be right, we will continue to grow by natural selection, survival of the fittest, or by design, until we use most or all of our brain (we only use 10% today).

Our useless appendages will wither away, our thought processes will increase a hundred fold, we will be able to use telekinesis (moving objects using thought), extra-sensory perception (read minds, tell the future), move around without the "infernal" combustion engine (the car), etc. Remember the song, "In the Year 2525"? Then, in time approaching infinite time, we will eventually progress (maybe it will be sooner, rather than later, as we see things happening in our age happen faster than hundreds of years ago) to the point that we can do a lot more than what we have seen in the movies, eg, Star Trek, 2001, A Space Odyssey, etc. We may not be able to create (only God does that) but we may have abilities to overcome the Time-Space Continuum and time travel, for example. We will do things, Lord willing, beyond our present stage of evolution. Keep in mind that the source of all creation is the ID, or God, and He has the where-with-all to send his Son, however He wants, so science and religion do not conflict, but only support His infinite capacity.

CHAPTER FOURTEEN
Universe # 429

My grandfather and I talked about time being a power in itself. I reminisce about him and how we discussed these things in the 50s. Since then, many films have portrayed time travel, as in H.G. Wells' "The Time Machine" and Michael J. Fox has given us levity with the "Back to the Future" trilogy. But consider this: eternity has already happened, since if time goes back as well as forward infinitely, there has already been an eternity of time before us. The absurdity of this brings to mind a new concept. Did you ever look at a photograph? It captures an instant in time but does not have one facet: MOTION. Therefore let us imagine the following: The Designer is outside of time. When you die, your spirit talks with Him and you want to see your past life, for example. He takes a roll of film off the shelf. "You lived in Universe # 429," he says.

He rolls the film. You see a MOTION picture. This is where time is. The roll of film may be starting with the "Big Bang" and ending with the collapse of the stars into a Singularity, the "God" Particle. When all the atoms are packed in, a point in time (an instant, approaching infinitely small, like the point on the line tangent to the parabola) is reached when motion stops. End of Universe # 429.

Time only exists where there is motion. The spirits can see the past present and future, all because it is rolled up in the catalogued Universe films.

Back to the photograph. It shows all you mind can conjure up, as in, "a picture is worth a thousand words". Yet, it stops time. The mind goes on, but the light that made the picture was captured and time has stopped. The Intelligent Designer may be observing the roll of cosmic film called Universe # 429 in the same way we are observing the photograph of Aunt Gertrude. Only He can start the projector.

CHAPTER FIFTEEN

The Nature of Evil in Infinity

Atheists say that, in infinity, an intelligent designer cannot be all-good and all powerful at the same time. The argument goes like this: Assume Evil happens. If the designer of the universe was all good, He could not be all powerful, because He would prevent that evil; conversely, if evil exists and the designer was all powerful, it could not be all good, because He has the power to destroy evil, but chooses not to.

Let us take an different approach. Are that all natural disasters in your life taken together, all famines, floods, earthquakes, fires, diseases, even death itself evil? They are horrendously painful, like giving birth. In terms of eternity or infinity, life is less than an instant anyway, just like a point in time. But is pain evil? Or is it a warning that something greater is occurring? Does a mustard seed feel pain when it sprouts and becomes an oak tree?

Witchcraft was once thought to be an evil power. (18)Women were burned at the stake by good God-fearing people because of this condition. Was that evil?

We all know ourselves that the death of a child, or a birth defect, or cancer, are extremely painful. If we were not intelligently conscious of them, we may feel them as sorrowful/pain, but would we think of them as evil?

In the animal kingdom, the wolverine is said to be the only animal that kills for pleasure rather than food. Tigers visciously kill their prey. Monkeys gang up on another breed, chase it down, and kill and eat it. Is this evil?

Do we attribute evil to these acts in humans? This comes to the point of the Biblical "Garden of Eden". Adam and Eve are said to have been tempted by the devil, fallen Angel Lucifer, to eat of the fruit of the Tree of the Knowledge of Good and Evil. Their original sin was "egoistic pride". Their sin was messing with nature trying to replace God. The epitomy of the human race, later known as Jesus, links our consciousness with the Deity in what Freud called "Super Ego", doing deeds not selfishly but for the good of all creation. He even suffered incalculable ego pain by knowingly being humiliated and killed by the very creatures he created through his Father (New Testament, Holy Bible).

Knowing we have a spiritual consciousness, we now have to use our FREE WILL to be worthy of heaven, instead of it being handed to us on a silver platter.

n math, physics, and even sociology, there exists a "standard deviation", whereby every large population has an abnormality at their extremes, ie. 1-2 % of humans have abnormalties, are super intelligent, or are otherwise deviant from the rest. The most painful deviations are those that cause us to suffer emotionally, but are unavoidable because the universe is built that way. Every star gets born but must die, every life has pain. But since 98% of our universe is truly wonderful, even though there are clouds, creation is still worthwhile. Deviations are a fact of life. A German saying, "Wo gehobelt wird, fallen Spaehne" means, "Where you smooth out wood, you get splinters". Perhaps in the long run, the bad in our lives give us redemption. The "splinters" can be used to soak up the oil spills! But are they evil?

I submit that the only evil on this earth that exists (not counting fallen angels) is in the human mind, in our consciousness. It is that which is willful in intention, to transgress nature, arrogantly anti-creation, destructive. We became conscious of evil when we became human. This biblically, came when we discovered we were naked.

In humans, all religions have acts they think of as "sin". The Ten Commandments of Judeo-Christian religion list "sins". Sins are evil. The Commandments have been banned from being posted in our public schools due to the concept of Separation of Church and State. But nevertheless, here they are:

1. "I am the Lord, thy God, thou shalt not have strange Gods before me"

2. "Thou shalt not take the Name of the Lord thy God in vain"

3. "Remember to keep holy the Lord's day"

4. "Honor thy father and thy mother"

5. "Thou shalt not kill"

6. "Thou shalt not commit adultery"

7. "Thou shalt not steal"

8. "Thou shalt not bear false witness against thy neighbor"

9. "Thou shalt not covet thy neighbor's wife"

10. "Thou shalt not covet thy neighbor's goods"

These sins all violate what a philosopher named Emmanuel Kant once called, the Categorical Imperative- "if everyone in the world performed a certain act, would the world be better or worse"?

Outside of this physical world, evil in essence could exist as a metaphysical being, the Devil, along with other angels. The evil thoughts that exist as part of us must be burned away, strained off, annihilated from our essence and must not be allowed in the next dimension, the "good".

CHAPTER SIXTEEN

Epilogue

We have discussed the concepts of eternity, evil, time, witchcraft, evolution, spirits, science and religion. The only conclusion is what we previously said of Aristotle, Greek philosopher, hundreds of years B.C.: "The only thing I know is that I don't know ". We would only hope that what another greater Thinker once said, is true, that there is the existence of an eternal reward in "Nirvana", "Heaven", or "after-life". In this earth, the Alpha and the Omega are shielded from our eyes, perhaps for our own good. Maybe our life is a kind of a training film, or as a proving grounds, to test our good from our unworthy traits. Many stories are told about people who have almost passed to the "other side", and come back to relate what they have seen. These people have no collusion, but all have a common thread: a light, a tunnel, a great expectation. Let us "hope" that their "faith" can lead to our greatest desire, that the Being that gave us these longings has the "charity" to not let it all end here. History repeats itself they say. But in order to be "gods", we will have to be as holy as "Buddha". Remember the Commandment "I am the Lord thy God, thou shalt not have strange gods before me. The greatest sin was Lucifer's, the sin of Pride. Let us realize that whatever was the cause, Somebody wanted to share creation with us and communicate. The Word was God, and dwelt among us. (19)

We have noted that there are explanations of the infinite from people like Confucius, Buddha, Aristotle, Socrates, Plato, Galileo, Newton, Goethe, Heisenberg, Einstein, and lately, Hawking. But only one Person has all the answers — JESUS.

Like the Beatles sang: "All you need is Love"(20).

Infinity, here we come!

About the Author:

Stephen Janusz was born in Buffalo N.Y. in 1946, another baby boomer. He worked with his grandfather on his concept of a "perpetual motion" machine in the 1950's. That is where he got his interest in "infinity". He went to a Catholic Grammar School, Catholic High School and finally Canisius College in Buffalo NY. This is where he minored in Philosophy. Being taught by Jesuits, he incorporated his concepts of the Metaphysical and Natural science.

After graduation, he became a special weapons Officer for the U.S. Army in 1968.Since then, he has travelled extensively in Europe from 1972 to 2010, and attended Troy State University, overseas branch, where he received a Master's Degree in Human Resource Management in 1977. He taught Mathematics for Big Bend Community College and Central Texas College overseas.

Isolde Janusz, his wife, was born Schoenenberg, Germany, and worked for Armed Forces from 1967 to 2004. She was one of nine children who lived through the Cold War and computerized government programs in logistics throughout her career. She typed and translated for Dr. Paul Wallerstein (deceased) in the making of his book, The AIDS Dilemma (1988).

Bibliography

1. The Grand Design, Stephen Hawking and Leonard Mlodinow, Bantam Books, N.Y., 2010

2. Relativity De Mystified, David McMahon, McGraw Hill, 2006

3. Six Roads from Newton, Edward Speyer, John Wiley & Sons, Inc., 1994

4. Physics of the Impossible, Michael Kaku, First Anchor Books Edition, April 2009

5. The Bible, Public Domain, New Testament, Matthew, Mark, Luke, and John

6. Access Science, McGraw Hill, 2008

7. AIDS-DAS DILEMMA, Paul Wallerstein, 1988, Rombach Press, GMBH

8. Mysteries of the Ancient Americas", Readers's Digest Association, NY, 1986.

9. Calculus With Analytical Geometry, Taylor, Angus E, Prentice-Hall, Inc, 1959,

10. Abbey Road, Album, The Beatles, 1966

11. "Origin of Life", Encyclopedia of Evolution, Oxford Press, 2002

12. Blog, Internet, Physics and Consciousness, Quantum Interconnectedness, Nature and Mind, Body and Spirit. StarStuffs, 2012

13. Alan Guth, "the Inflationary Universe" Page 271-276, date and Publisher?

14. Stephen Hawking, "A Brief History of Time, from the Big Bang to Black Holes" page 136, Date and Publisher

15. Physics of the Impossible, Michael Kaku, First Anchor Books Edition, April 2009

16. Origin of Life", Encyclopedia of Evolution, Oxford Press, 2002, p.846

17. Endless Universe" Steinhardt Paul and Turik Neil, "Beyond the Big Bang" May 29, 2007, Kindle Edition Random House, Cyclic Universe

18. steve18 "Science News Edition", May 28, 2008, Society for Science and the Public, 2008 McGraw Hill, 2011

19. "The Bible", Public Domain, New Testament, Matthew, Mark, Luke, and John,

20. "Death Receptor Signalling",Golkes, Lavrik A. and Krammer, D. J Cell 188 265=267, 2007

21. "Cosmology", Bondi, A. 2nd Edition Cambridge University Press 1960

22. "Mysteries of the Ancient Americas", Readers Digest Association, NY, 1986 P, 20

23. "Psychosis", Hoffman Ralph E, In Access Science, McGraw Hill 2008 www.access science.com

24. Blog, Internet, Physics and Consciousness, Quantum Interconnectedness, Nature and Mind, Body and Spirit. StarStuffs, 2012

25. Introduction to Real Analysis", R.G. Bartle and D.R. Sherbert, CLD, McGraw Hill. 1999

Footnotes:

1. "The Grand Design", Stephen Hawking and Leonard Mlodinow, Bantam Books, 2010, p.102

2. Relativity DeMystified", David McMahon, McGraw Hill,2006, p.181

3. Blog, Internet, Physics and Consciousness, Quantum Interconnectedness, Nature and Mind, Body and Spirit. StarStuffs, 2012

4. "Calculus With Analytical Geometry," Angus E. Taylor, Prentice- Hall, Inc, 1959,

5. "Slow Time Scale", Access Science, Mcgraw Hill. 2011 https : access science.com

6. Physics of the Impossible, Michael Kaku, First Anchor Books Edition, April 2009

7. Blog, Internet, Edey Caldwell-Sanders, "Quantum Healing Utilizing Master Clinical

8. Blog, Internet, Skylark and Funderberg, "Can Science and Religion Coexist ?", 2012

9. "Origin Of Life", Encyclopedia of Evolution, Oxford Press, 2002. P 486.

10. "Mysteries of the Ancient Americas", Readers Digest Association, NY, 1986 P, 20

11. "Endless Universe" Steinhardt Paul and Turik Neil, "Beyond the Big Bang" May 29, 2007, Kindle Edition Random House, Cyclic Universe

12. "Cosmology", Bondi, A. 2nd Edition Cambridge University Press 1960

13. "The Bible", New Testament, Chapter 24, Matthew

14. "Death Receptor Signaling",Golkes, Lavrik A. and Krammer, D. J Cell 188 265=267, 2007

15. Stephen Hawking, "A Brief History of Time, from the Big Bang to Black Holes" page 136, Date and Publisher

16. "Mysteries of the Ancient Americas", Readers Digest Association, NY, 1986 P, 20

17. "The Bible", Public Domain, New Testament, Matthew, Mark, Luke, and John

18. "Psychosis", Hoffman Ralph E, In Access Science, McGraw Hill 2008 www.access science.com

19. "The Bible", Public Domain, New Testament, Matthew, Mark, Luke, and John

20. "Abby Road", Album, The Beatles", 1969

Acknowledgements

For my son-in-law, who initiated the Gmail that started the book on its way: **Nishan Claussen**

For my daughter, who looked throughout history to find religion: **Jennifer Claussen**

For my grandson, who will always be cherished as the crown jewel: **Josiah Claussen**

Persons who were inspirational to the making of this book and deserve acknowledging:

Tyler D. Carouthers-Childs

Bradley M. Collinsworth

Charles D. Lipscomb

Eric A. Cole

Kaleb M. Yatrofsky

Justin M. Williams

Special acknowledgement to my friends who edited, produced, and directed this book for world dissemination:

Tim L. Schoon

Karl-Heinz Schoon

For your thoughts and notes:

For your thoughts and notes:

For your thoughts and notes: